THIS BOOK BELONGS TO

_____

_____

START DATE

| MONTH | DAY | YEAR |

SHE READS TRUTH™

ISBN 978-1-946282-02-6

Unless otherwise noted, all Scripture quotations are taken from the HCSB®, Copyright © 1999, 2000, 2002, 2003, 2009 by Holman Bible Publishers. Used by permission. HCSB® is a federally registered trademark of Holman Bible Publishers.

Scripture quotations marked ESV are from ESV® Bible (The Holy Bible, English Standard Version®), copyright © 2001 by Crossway, a publishing ministry of Good News Publishers. Used by permission. All rights reserved.

Scripture quotations marked NIV are taken from the Holy Bible, New International Version®, NIV®. Copyright © 1973, 1978, 1984, 2011 by Biblica, Inc.™ Used by permission of Zondervan. All rights reserved worldwide. www.zondervan.com The "NIV" and "New International Version" are trademarks registered in the United States Patent and Trademark Office by Biblica, Inc.™

Photography © 2017 by Ashley Glass (4, 12, 16, 24, 44, 50, 56, 64), Kellie Beth Scott (27, 30, 48, 66), Alyssa Valletta (22, 60), and Cymone Wilder (cover). Used by permission.

MAKING ROOM

A STUDY OF BIBLICAL HOSPITALITY

SHE READS TRUTH

Nashville, Tennessee

Therefore welcome one another as Christ
has welcomed you, for the glory of God.
– Romans 15:7 ESV

One evening last fall I was invited to a friend's house to pray. The agenda was simple enough: eat snacks and mingle, settle in to spend time alone in prayer, then encourage each other.

I'm not always comfortable with group events, and nine times out of ten I'll choose being home and quiet over a social gathering, especially on a weeknight. But this time I went. Mostly compelled by an opportunity to catch up with some friends and the possibility of a slice of cheesecake, I reassured myself that the tender-heart time wouldn't last too long.

Several months later I cannot recall how the food tasted or what shoes I wore or how awkward I felt. But I clearly remember how the Lord used that gathering to soften my heart in a very specific way. That night, in the quiet of the solo prayer time, the Holy Spirit impressed upon my heart just two words: *make room.*

In the days that followed, I considered the different ways I could make room: in my heart, on my calendar, in my home. I thought about who I could make room for: the new women moving to our burgeoning city, the people I know who need more than they have to offer, and the guy who definitely eased his way in front of me in line at the concession stand last weekend. But even before any of that, I can make room for my Lord, who promises me His presence whether or not I take time to be present with Him.

As I penciled down a list, I realized all the ways people had already made room for me:

Here is my time—it's yours now.

Here is this meal—I want you to be nourished.

Here is my forgiveness—I know what a gift is to be forgiven.

Here is this space to sit—I'd rather you have rest than me.

Here I am entering into your sorrow—I was comfortable, but you need comfort more than me.

Even more extravagantly than the hospitality offered to me by others is that offered by the Father Himself:

I was an orphan—He called me His daughter.

I was a foreigner—He made me a citizen.

My sin made me unclean like a leper—He did not cast me out.

Hospitality, I am learning, is often untidy and almost always inconvenient. But making room is not about my own comfort. It's about taking something I presume is mine, and offering it to someone else.

Not long after my evening of cheesecake, the She Reads Truth team began to talk about creating a Bible reading plan on the topic of hospitality. We looked at all the types of people Jesus made room for—neighbors, the poor, His betrayers, strangers, children, and so many more. It was a mark of His ministry: offering Himself to others and to the Father.

This book is personal for our team. As we prepare for this study, we are realizing that God makes us living testimonies of Christ's life by this Truth: "we love because He first loved us" (1 John 4:19). In being inconvenienced and uncomfortable and messy, we are finding a nearness with God—because Jesus was these things and more on our behalf. We are learning to make room for others because while we were still sinners, room was made for us.

Thanks be to God.

Raechel

Raechel Myers
EDITOR-IN-CHIEF

HOW TO STUDY WITH THE ONLINE COMMUNITY

For added community and conversation, join us in the **Making Room: A Study of Biblical Hospitality** reading plan on the She Reads Truth app or on SheReadsTruth.com.

Have a "He" in your life—a brother, father, husband, friend? Invite him to join you by visiting HeReadsTruth.com or the He Reads Truth app, or by picking up the guy version of this book at ShopHeReadsTruth.com.

She Reads Truth is a community of women dedicated to reading the Word of God every day. The Bible is living and active, breathed out by God, and we confidently hold it higher than anything we can do or say. This book focuses primarily on Scripture, with bonus resources to facilitate deeper engagement with God's Word.

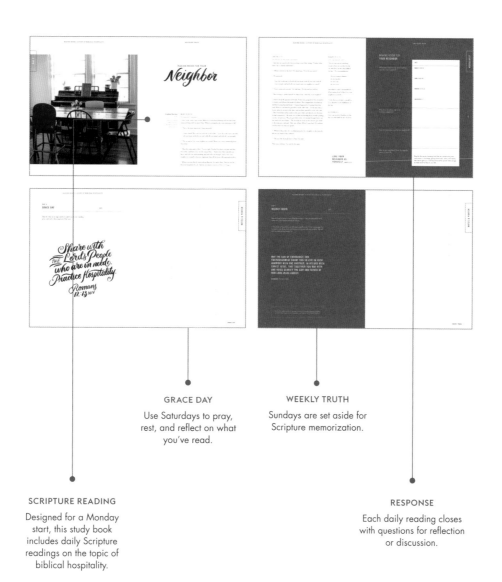

GRACE DAY

Use Saturdays to pray, rest, and reflect on what you've read.

WEEKLY TRUTH

Sundays are set aside for Scripture memorization.

SCRIPTURE READING

Designed for a Monday start, this study book includes daily Scripture readings on the topic of biblical hospitality.

RESPONSE

Each daily reading closes with questions for reflection or discussion.

TABLE OF CONTENTS

"Let the little children come to Me." MARK 10:13

Put on love—the
perfect bond of unity.

COLOSSIANS 3:14

PAGE
60

PAGE
38

ROMANS 15:7 ESV

Therefore welcome one another as Christ has welcomed you, for the glory of God

MAKING ROOM FOR

Others

Scripture Reading

———

Romans 12:3–8
Acts 15:6–21
Galatians 3:27–29

ROMANS 12:3–8

MANY GIFTS BUT ONE BODY

[3] For by the grace given to me, I tell everyone among you not to think of himself more highly than he should think. Instead, think sensibly, as God has distributed a measure of faith to each one. [4] Now as we have many parts in one body, and all the parts do not have the same function, [5] in the same way we who are many are one body in Christ and individually members of one another. [6] According to the grace given to us, we have different gifts:

If prophecy,
use it according to the standard of one's faith;
[7] if service, in service;
if teaching, in teaching;
[8] if exhorting, in exhortation;
giving, with generosity;
leading, with diligence;
showing mercy, with cheerfulness.

ACTS 15:6–21

THE JERUSALEM COUNCIL

[6] Then the apostles and the elders assembled to consider this matter. [7] After there had been much debate, Peter stood up and said to them: "Brothers, you are aware that in the early days God made a choice among you, that by my mouth the Gentiles would hear the gospel message and believe. [8] And God, who knows the heart, testified to them by giving the Holy Spirit, just as He also did to us. [9] He made no distinction between us and them, cleansing their hearts by faith. [10] Now then, why are you testing God by putting a yoke on the disciples' necks that neither our ancestors nor we have been able to bear? [11] On the contrary, we believe we are saved through the grace of the Lord Jesus in the same way they are."

[12] Then the whole assembly fell silent and listened to Barnabas and Paul describing all the signs and wonders God had done through them among the Gentiles. [13] After they stopped speaking, James responded: "Brothers, listen to me! [14] Simeon has reported how God first intervened to take from the Gentiles a people for His name. [15] And the words of the prophets agree with this, as it is written:

> [16] After these things I will return
> and rebuild David's fallen tent.
> I will rebuild its ruins
> and set it up again,
> [17] so the rest of humanity
> may seek the Lord—
> even all the Gentiles
> who are called by My name,
> declares the Lord who does these things,
> [18] known from long ago.

[19] Therefore, in my judgment, we should not cause difficulties for those among the Gentiles who turn to God, [20] but instead we should write to them to abstain from things polluted by idols, from sexual immorality, from eating anything that has been strangled, and from blood. [21] For since ancient times, Moses has had those who proclaim him in every city, and every Sabbath day he is read aloud in the synagogues."

GALATIANS 3:27–29

SONS AND HEIRS

[27] For as many of you as have been baptized into Christ have put on Christ like a garment. [28] There is no Jew or Greek, slave or free, male or female; for you are all one in Christ Jesus. [29] And if you belong to Christ, then you are Abraham's seed, heirs according to the promise.

ACCORDING TO
THE GRACE GIVEN
TO US, WE HAVE
DIFFERENT GIFTS...
ROMANS 12:6

MAKING ROOM FOR **OTHERS**

DATE:

What does Scripture say about making room for others?

ROMANS 12:3–8

ACTS 15:6–21

GALATIANS 3:27–29

Why does Scripture urge us to welcome others?

How can we make room for people who are different from us?

Did God bring anyone to mind as you read? Think of that person's name or write it down.

Pray for this person, thanking God that He created every man and woman in His image, giving them worth, value, and dignity. Ask God to give you a soft heart toward this person and courage to make room for them in your life.

MAKING ROOM FOR YOUR

Neighbor

MARK 12:28–34

THE PRIMARY COMMANDS

28 One of the scribes approached. When he heard them debating and saw that Jesus answered them well, he asked Him, "Which command is the most important of all?"

29 "This is the most important," Jesus answered:

> Listen, Israel! The Lord our God, the Lord is One. 30 Love the Lord your God with all your heart, with all your soul, with all your mind, and with all your strength.

31 "The second is: Love your neighbor as yourself. There is no other command greater than these."

32 Then the scribe said to Him, "You are right, Teacher! You have correctly said that He is One, and there is no one else except Him. 33 And to love Him with all your heart, with all your understanding, and with all your strength, and to love your neighbor as yourself, is far more important than all the burnt offerings and sacrifices."

34 When Jesus saw that he answered intelligently, He said to him, "You are not far from the kingdom of God." And no one dared to question Him any longer.

LUKE 10:25–37

THE PARABLE OF THE GOOD SAMARITAN

[25] Just then an expert in the law stood up to test Him, saying, "Teacher, what must I do to inherit eternal life?"

[26] "What is written in the law?" He asked him. "How do you read it?"

[27] He answered:

> Love the Lord your God with all your heart, with all your soul, with all your strength, and with all your mind; and your neighbor as yourself.

[28] "You've answered correctly," He told him. "Do this and you will live."

[29] But wanting to justify himself, he asked Jesus, "And who is my neighbor?"

[30] Jesus took up the question and said: "A man was going down from Jerusalem to Jericho and fell into the hands of robbers. They stripped him, beat him up, and fled, leaving him half dead. [31] A priest happened to be going down that road. When he saw him, he passed by on the other side. [32] In the same way, a Levite, when he arrived at the place and saw him, passed by on the other side. [33] But a Samaritan on his journey came up to him, and when he saw the man, he had compassion. [34] He went over to him and bandaged his wounds, pouring on olive oil and wine. Then he put him on his own animal, brought him to an inn, and took care of him. [35] The next day he took out two denarii, gave them to the innkeeper, and said, 'Take care of him. When I come back I'll reimburse you for whatever extra you spend.'

[36] "Which of these three do you think proved to be a neighbor to the man who fell into the hands of the robbers?"

[37] "The one who showed mercy to him," he said.

Then Jesus told him, "Go and do the same."

ROMANS 13:8–10

LOVE, OUR PRIMARY DUTY

[8] Do not owe anyone anything, except to love one another, for the one who loves another has fulfilled the law. [9] The commandments:

> Do not commit adultery;
> do not murder;
> do not steal;
> do not covet;

and whatever other commandment— all are summed up by this: Love your neighbor as yourself.

[10] Love does no wrong to a neighbor. Love, therefore, is the fulfillment of the law.

GALATIANS 6:2

Carry one another's burdens; in this way you will fulfill the law of Christ.

"LOVE YOUR NEIGHBOR AS YOURSELF." MARK 12:31

MAKING ROOM FOR
YOUR NEIGHBOR

DATE:

What does Scripture say about making
room for your neighbor?

MARK 12:28–34

LUKE 10:25–37

ROMANS 13:8–10

GALATIANS 6:2

Why does Scripture urge us to
welcome neighbors?

How can we make room for our neighbors?

Who is your neighbor? Think of a specific
person in your life.

Pray for this person, thanking God that He created every man
and woman in His image, giving them worth, value, and dignity.
Ask God to give you a soft heart toward this person and courage
to make room for them in your life.

JAMES 2:13

MAKING ROOM FOR THE

Poor

DAY 3

DEUTERONOMY 15:11

For there will never cease to be poor people in the land; that is why I am commanding you, "You must willingly open your hand to your afflicted and poor brother in your land."

1 SAMUEL 2:7–8

7 The LORD brings poverty and gives wealth;
He humbles and He exalts.
8 He raises the poor from the dust
and lifts the needy from the garbage pile.
He seats them with noblemen
and gives them a throne of honor.
For the foundations of the earth are the Lord's;
He has set the world on them.

PROVERBS 22:9

A generous person will be blessed,
for he shares his food with the poor.

JAMES 2:1–13

THE SIN OF FAVORITISM

[1] My brothers, do not show favoritism as you hold on to the faith in our glorious Lord Jesus Christ. [2] For example, a man comes into your meeting wearing a gold ring and dressed in fine clothes, and a poor man dressed in dirty clothes also comes in. [3] If you look with favor on the man wearing the fine clothes and say, "Sit here in a good place," and yet you say to the poor man, "Stand over there," or, "Sit here on the floor by my footstool," [4] haven't you discriminated among yourselves and become judges with evil thoughts?

[5] Listen, my dear brothers: Didn't God choose the poor in this world to be rich in faith and heirs of the kingdom that He has promised to those who love Him? [6] Yet you dishonored that poor man. Don't the rich oppress you and drag you into the courts? [7] Don't they blaspheme the noble name that was pronounced over you at your baptism?

[8] Indeed, if you keep the royal law prescribed in the Scripture, Love your neighbor as yourself, you are doing well. [9] But if you show favoritism, you commit sin and are convicted by the law as transgressors. [10] For whoever keeps the entire law, yet fails in one point, is guilty of breaking it all. [11] For He who said, Do not commit adultery, also said, Do not murder. So if you do not commit adultery, but you do murder, you are a lawbreaker.

[12] Speak and act as those who will be judged by the law of freedom. [13] For judgment is without mercy to the one who hasn't shown mercy. Mercy triumphs over judgment.

1 TIMOTHY 6:17–19

INSTRUCTIONS TO THE RICH

[17] Instruct those who are rich in the present age not to be arrogant or to set their hope on the uncertainty of wealth, but on God, who richly provides us with all things to enjoy. [18] Instruct them to do what is good, to be rich in good works, to be generous, willing to share, [19] storing up for themselves a good reserve for the age to come, so that they may take hold of life that is real.

1 JOHN 3:17–20

[17] If anyone has this world's goods and sees his brother in need but closes his eyes to his need—how can God's love reside in him?

[18] Little children, we must not love with word or speech, but with truth and action. [19] This is how we will know we belong to the truth and will convince our conscience in His presence, [20] even if our conscience condemns us, that God is greater than our conscience, and He knows all things.

MAKING ROOM FOR **THE POOR**

DATE:

What does Scripture say about making room for the poor?

DEUTERONOMY 15:11

1 SAMUEL 2:7–8

1 TIMOTHY 6:17–19

JAMES 2:1–13

Why does Scripture urge us to welcome the poor?

How can we make room for those in spiritual or financial poverty?

Did God bring anyone to mind as you read? Think of that person's name or write it down.

Pray for this person, thanking God that He created every man and woman in His image, giving them worth, value, and dignity. Ask God to give you a soft heart toward this person and courage to make room for them in your life.

DAY 4

MAKING ROOM FOR THE
Self-Righteous

Scripture Reading

———

Matthew 7:1–5
Matthew 23:37–39
Luke 15:11–32
Luke 18:9–14
Romans 2:1–11
Romans 3:9–23

MATTHEW 7:1–5

DO NOT JUDGE

[1] "Do not judge, so that you won't be judged. [2] For with the judgment you use, you will be judged, and with the measure you use, it will be measured to you. [3] Why do you look at the speck in your brother's eye but don't notice the log in your own eye? [4] Or how can you say to your brother, 'Let me take the speck out of your eye,' and look, there's a log in your eye? [5] Hypocrite! First take the log out of your eye, and then you will see clearly to take the speck out of your brother's eye."

MATTHEW 23:37–39

JESUS' LAMENTATION OVER JERUSALEM

[37] "Jerusalem, Jerusalem! She who kills the prophets and stones those who are sent to her. How often I wanted to gather your children together, as a hen gathers her chicks under her wings, yet you were not willing! [38] See, your house is left to you desolate. [39] For I tell you, you will never see Me again until you say, 'He who comes in the name of the Lord is the blessed One'!"

LUKE 15:11–32

THE PARABLE OF THE LOST SON

[11] He also said: "A man had two sons. [12] The younger of them said to his father, 'Father, give me the share of the estate I have coming to me.' So he distributed the assets to them. [13] Not many days later, the younger son gathered together all he had and traveled to a distant country, where he squandered his estate in foolish living. [14] After he had spent everything, a severe famine struck that country, and he had nothing. [15] Then he went to work for one of the citizens of that country, who sent him into his fields to feed pigs. [16] He longed to eat his fill from the carob pods the pigs were eating, but no one would give him any. [17] When he came to his senses, he said, 'How many of my father's hired hands have more than enough food, and here I am dying of hunger! [18] I'll get up, go to my father, and say to him, Father, I have sinned against heaven and in your sight. [19] I'm no longer worthy to be called your son. Make me like one of your hired hands.' [20] So he got up and went to his father. But while the son was still a long way off, his father saw him and was filled with compassion. He ran, threw his arms around his neck, and kissed him. [21] The son said to him, 'Father, I have sinned against heaven and in your sight. I'm no longer worthy to be called your son.'

[22] "But the father told his slaves, 'Quick! Bring out the best robe and put it on him; put a ring on his finger and sandals on his feet. [23] Then bring the fattened calf and slaughter it, and let's celebrate with a feast, [24] because this son of mine was dead and is alive again; he was lost and is found!' So they began to celebrate.

[25] "Now his older son was in the field; as he came near the house, he heard music and dancing. [26] So he summoned one of the servants and asked what these things meant. [27] 'Your brother is here,' he told him, 'and your father has slaughtered the fattened calf because he has him back safe and sound.'

[28] "Then he became angry and didn't want to go in. So his father came out and pleaded with him. [29] But he replied to his father, 'Look, I have been slaving many years for you, and I have never disobeyed your orders, yet you never gave me a young goat so I could celebrate with my friends. [30] But when this son of yours came, who has devoured your assets with prostitutes, you slaughtered the fattened calf for him.'

[31] "'Son,' he said to him, 'you are always with me, and everything I have is yours. [32] But we had to celebrate and rejoice, because this brother of yours was dead and is alive again; he was lost and is found.'"

LUKE 18:9–14

THE PARABLE OF THE PHARISEE AND THE TAX COLLECTOR

[9] He also told this parable to some who trusted in themselves that they were righteous and looked down on everyone else: [10] "Two men went up to the temple complex to pray, one a Pharisee and the other a tax collector. [11] The Pharisee took his stand and was praying like this: 'God, I thank You that I'm not like other people —greedy, unrighteous, adulterers, or even like this tax collector. [12] I fast twice a week; I give a tenth of everything I get.'

[13] "But the tax collector, standing far off, would not even raise his eyes to heaven but kept striking his chest and saying, 'God, turn Your wrath from me—a sinner!' [14] I tell you, this one went down to his house justified rather than the other; because everyone who exalts himself will be humbled, but the one who humbles himself will be exalted."

ROMANS 2:1–11

GOD'S RIGHTEOUS JUDGMENT

[1] Therefore, any one of you who judges is without excuse. For when you judge another, you condemn yourself, since you, the judge, do the same things. [2] We know that God's judgment on those who do such things is based on the truth. [3] Do you really think—anyone of you who judges those who do such things yet do the same—that you will escape God's judgment? [4] Or do you despise the riches of His kindness, restraint, and patience, not recognizing that God's kindness is intended to lead you to repentance? [5] But because of your hardness and unrepentant heart you are storing up wrath for yourself in the day of wrath, when God's righteous judgment is revealed. [6] He will repay each one according to his works: [7] eternal life to those who by persistence in doing good seek glory, honor, and immortality; [8] but wrath and indignation to those who are self-seeking and disobey the truth but are obeying unrighteousness; [9] affliction and distress for every human being who does evil, first to the Jew, and also to the Greek; [10] but glory, honor, and peace for everyone who does what is good, first to the Jew, and also to the Greek. [11] There is no favoritism with God.

ROMANS 3:9–23

THE WHOLE WORLD GUILTY BEFORE GOD

[9] What then? Are we any better? Not at all! For we have previously charged that both Jews and Gentiles are all under sin, [10] as it is written:

There is no one righteous, not even one.
[11] There is no one who understands;
there is no one who seeks God.
[12] All have turned away;
all alike have become useless.
There is no one who does what is good,
not even one.
[13] Their throat is an open grave;
they deceive with their tongues.
Vipers' venom is under their lips.
[14] Their mouth is full of cursing and bitterness.
[15] Their feet are swift to shed blood;
[16] ruin and wretchedness are in their paths,
[17] and the path of peace they have not known.
[18] There is no fear of God before their eyes.

[19] Now we know that whatever the law says speaks to those who are subject to the law, so that every mouth may be shut and the whole world may become subject to God's judgment. [20] For no one will be justified in His sight by the works of the law, because the knowledge of sin comes through the law.

GOD'S RIGHTEOUSNESS THROUGH FAITH

[21] But now, apart from the law, God's righteousness has been revealed—attested by the Law and the Prophets [22] —that is, God's righteousness through faith in Jesus Christ, to all who believe, since there is no distinction. [23] For all have sinned and fall short of the glory of God.

"HOW OFTEN I WANTED TO GATHER YOUR CHILDREN TOGETHER, AS A HEN GATHERS HER CHICKS UNDER HER WINGS, YET YOU WERE NOT WILLING!" MATTHEW 23:37

MAKING ROOM FOR
THE SELF-RIGHTEOUS

DATE:

What does Scripture say about making room for the self-righteous?

MATTHEW 7:1–5

LUKE 18:9–14

ROMANS 2:1–11

ROMANS 3:9–23

Why does Scripture urge us to welcome the self-righteous?

How can we make room for those who are self-righteous?

Consider the ways that you are self-righteous. Repent, and thank God for His grace that covers even your pride.

-
-
-

Pray, thanking God that He created you in His image, giving you worth, value, and dignity. Ask God to teach you to make room for people other than yourself.

MAKING ROOM FOR YOUR

Betrayers

EXODUS 23:4–5

4 "If you come across your enemy's stray ox or donkey, you must return it to him.

5 If you see the donkey of someone who hates you lying helpless under its load, and you want to refrain from helping it, you must help with it."

MATTHEW 18:15–20

RESTORING A BROTHER

15 "If your brother sins against you, go and rebuke him in private. If he listens to you, you have won your brother. 16 But if he won't listen, take one or two more with you, so that by the testimony of two or three witnesses every fact may be established. 17 If he pays no attention to them, tell the church. But if he doesn't pay attention even to the church, let him be like an unbeliever and a tax collector to you. 18 I assure you: Whatever you bind on earth is already bound in heaven, and whatever you loose on earth is already loosed in heaven. 19 Again, I assure you: If two of you on earth agree about any matter that you pray for, it will be done for you by My Father in heaven. 20 For where two or three are gathered together in My name, I am there among them."

LUKE 6:27–36

LOVE YOUR ENEMIES

[27] "But I say to you who listen: Love your enemies, do what is good to those who hate you, [28] bless those who curse you, pray for those who mistreat you. [29] If anyone hits you on the cheek, offer the other also. And if anyone takes away your coat, don't hold back your shirt either. [30] Give to everyone who asks you, and from one who takes your things, don't ask for them back. [31] Just as you want others to do for you, do the same for them. [32] If you love those who love you, what credit is that to you? Even sinners love those who love them. [33] If you do what is good to those who are good to you, what credit is that to you? Even sinners do that. [34] And if you lend to those from whom you expect to receive, what credit is that to you? Even sinners lend to sinners to be repaid in full. [35] But love your enemies, do what is good, and lend, expecting nothing in return. Then your reward will be great, and you will be sons of the Most High. For He is gracious to the ungrateful and evil. [36] Be merciful, just as your Father also is merciful."

JOHN 18:15–18

PETER DENIES JESUS

[15] Meanwhile, Simon Peter was following Jesus, as was another disciple. That disciple was an acquaintance of the high priest; so he went with Jesus into the high priest's courtyard. [16] But Peter remained standing outside by the door. So the other disciple, the one known to the high priest, went out and spoke to the girl who was the doorkeeper and brought Peter in.

[17] Then the slave girl who was the doorkeeper said to Peter, "You aren't one of this man's disciples too, are you?"

"I am not!" he said. [18] Now the slaves and the temple police had made a charcoal fire, because it was cold. They were standing there warming themselves, and Peter was standing with them, warming himself.

JOHN 21:15–19

JESUS' THREEFOLD RESTORATION OF PETER

[15] When they had eaten breakfast, Jesus asked Simon Peter, "Simon, son of John, do you love Me more than these?"

"Yes, Lord," he said to Him, "You know that I love You."

"Feed My lambs," He told him.

[16] A second time He asked him, "Simon, son of John, do you love Me?"

"Yes, Lord," he said to Him, "You know that I love You."

"Shepherd My sheep," He told him.

[17] He asked him the third time, "Simon, son of John, do you love Me?"

Peter was grieved that He asked him the third time, "Do you love Me?" He said, "Lord, You know everything! You know that I love You."

"Feed My sheep," Jesus said. [18] "I assure you: When you were young, you would tie your belt and walk wherever you wanted. But when you grow old, you will stretch out your hands and someone else will tie you and carry you where you don't want to go." [19] He said this to signify by what kind of death he would glorify God. After saying this, He told him, "Follow Me!"

COLOSSIANS 3:12–13

THE CHRISTIAN LIFE

[12] Therefore, God's chosen ones, holy and loved, put on heartfelt compassion, kindness, humility, gentleness, and patience, [13] accepting one another and forgiving one another if anyone has a complaint against another. Just as the Lord has forgiven you, so you must also forgive.

MAKING ROOM FOR
YOUR BETRAYERS

DATE:

What does Scripture say about making room for your betrayers?

EXODUS 23:4–5

LUKE 6:27–36

JOHN 21:15–19

COLOSSIANS 3:12–13

Why does Scripture urge us to welcome even our betrayers?

How can we make room for our betrayers?

Who is a specific person in your life who has betrayed you or someone you love? Think of that person's name or write it down.

Pray for this person, thanking God that He created every man and woman in His image, giving them worth, value, and dignity. Ask God to give you courage to forgive and make room for those who have hurt you.

THEY BROKE BREAD IN THEIR HOMES
AND ATE TOGETHER WITH GLAD AND
SINCERE HEARTS...

ACTS 2:46 NIV

MAKE ROOM AT YOUR TABLE

GRANDMA ROXY'S CHOCOLATE CHIP COOKIES
Roxanne Pennington

———

You can bake cookies, or you can bake Roxanne's cookies. We went through several recipes, baking and testing, and they were fine, but they weren't Roxanne's. She comes from a long line of baking women who make unbelievably soft and delicious cookies. They are truly worth writing home about.

Our own Roxanne at #SRThq memorized this recipe on a spring morning when she baked twelve dozen cookies for a funeral, side by side with her grandma, Roxy. The sweetness of cookies as a gift to that grieving family cemented in her mind the value of hospitality on the happy days and the sad.

SKILLET-TOASTED PENNE WITH BACON AND SPINACH
Raechel Myers

———

This is a rich, warm pasta dish made without even a hint of cream or milk. By treating the pasta like risotto and cooking it in chicken stock, the starch is released to become the sauce. Toasting the pasta before cooking it is less technical than it sounds, and adds a unique, nutty flavor and color. Adding spinach and oregano makes the dish fresh and bright—a great go-to for dinner guests.

Once all the prep is done, this penne requires 35 minutes of constant stirring. Those long 35 minutes are a gift! Instead of rushing them or wishing them away, use this time to pray for the people who will eat this meal you are preparing. Pray for them by name, and thank the Lord for teaching us to make room for one another.

GRANDMA ROXY'S CHOCOLATE CHIP COOKIES

2 cups Crisco®
1 ½ cups white sugar
1 ½ cups brown sugar
4 eggs
4 ½ cups flour
2 teaspoons salt
2 teaspoons baking soda
2 teaspoons vanilla
2 cups semi-sweet chocolate chips

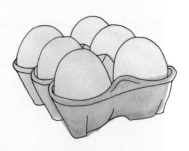

Preheat oven to 350°F.

Cream together Crisco, both sugars, & vanilla. Fold in the eggs individually & set aside.

In a separate bowl, sift together flour, salt, & baking soda.

Slowly incorporate dry ingredients into the wet ingredients. Mix in chocolate chips.

Spoon 1-inch dough balls onto a cookie sheet & bake until golden brown around the edges, about 10-12 minutes.

SKILLET-TOASTED PENNE WITH BACON AND SPINACH

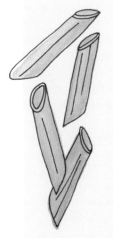

6 cups low-sodium chicken stock

3 tablespoons olive oil, divided

8 ounces dry penne pasta

6 ounces center-cut bacon (or turkey bacon), diced

2-4 shallots (or 1 medium yellow onion), coarse chopped

4 garlic cloves, sliced or minced

6 ounces baby spinach

1 tablespoon fresh lemon juice

½ teaspoon grated lemon rind

¼ teaspoon salt

1-2 ounces shredded parmesan cheese

Fresh oregano leaves

Bring stock to a simmer in saucepan (DO NOT BOIL). Keep warm over low heat.

Heat a wide, high-walled skillet over medium heat. Add 2 tablespoons oil to pan; swirl to coat. Add dry pasta & cook 5 minutes or until slightly browned, stirring frequently. Remove toasted pasta from pan.

Add remaining 1 tablespoon oil, shallots, garlic, & bacon to pan; cook 6 minutes on medium-high, or until bacon is browned. Remove bacon-shallot mixture from pan.

Reduce heat to medium-low. Return pasta to pan. Add stock, 1 cup at a time, stirring constantly until each portion of stock is nearly absorbed before adding the next (about 25 minutes total).

Stir in bacon-shallot mixture, lemon juice & rind, baby spinach, salt, & cheese. Garnish with fresh oregano leaves.

DAY 6
GRACE DAY

DATE:

Take this day as an opportunity to catch up on your reading,
pray, and rest in the presence of the Lord.

Share with the Lord's People who are in need. Practice Hospitality.

Romans 12:13 NIV

DAY 7
WEEKLY TRUTH

DATE:

Memorizing Scripture is one of the best ways to carry God-breathed truth, instruction, and reproof wherever we go.

In this study of hospitality we will memorize Romans 15:5–7, a passage that focuses on glorifying God and living in harmony with one another. We will start by memorizing verses 5–6.

MAY THE GOD OF ENDURANCE AND ENCOURAGEMENT GRANT YOU TO LIVE IN SUCH HARMONY WITH ONE ANOTHER, IN ACCORD WITH CHRIST JESUS, THAT TOGETHER YOU MAY WITH ONE VOICE GLORIFY THE GOD AND FATHER OF OUR LORD JESUS CHRIST.

ROMANS 15:5–6 ESV

Punch out the memory card for this passage in the back of your book and place it somewhere you'll see it often. As you memorize these verses, give thanks to God for the gift of His Word.

MAKING ROOM FOR

Widows AND Orphans

Scripture Reading

———

Isaiah 1:17
Psalm 68:4–6
John 14:15–18
1 Timothy 5:3–16
James 1:27

ISAIAH 1:17

Learn to do what is good.

Seek justice.

Correct the oppressor.

Defend the rights of the fatherless.

Plead the widow's cause.

PSALM 68:4–6

[4] Sing to God! Sing praises to His name.

Exalt Him who rides on the clouds —

His name is Yahweh—and rejoice before Him.

[5] God in His holy dwelling is

a father of the fatherless

and a champion of widows.

[6] God provides homes for those who are deserted.

He leads out the prisoners to prosperity,

but the rebellious live in a scorched land.

JOHN 14:15–18
ANOTHER COUNSELOR PROMISED

[15] "If you love Me, you will keep My commands. [16] And I will ask the Father, and He will give you another Counselor to be with you forever. [17] He is the Spirit of truth. The world is unable to receive Him because it doesn't see Him or know Him. But you do know Him, because He remains with you and will be in you. [18] I will not leave you as orphans; I am coming to you."

1 TIMOTHY 5:3–16
THE SUPPORT OF WIDOWS

[3] Support widows who are genuinely widows. [4] But if any widow has children or grandchildren, they must learn to practice godliness toward their own family first and to repay their parents, for this pleases God. [5] The real widow, left all alone, has put her hope in God and continues night and day in her petitions and prayers; [6] however, she who is self-indulgent is dead even while she lives. [7] Command this also, so they won't be blamed. [8] But if anyone does not provide for his own, that is his own household, he has denied the faith and is worse than an unbeliever.

[9] No widow should be placed on the official support list unless she is at least 60 years old, has been the wife of one husband, [10] and is well known for good works—that is, if she has brought up children, shown hospitality, washed the saints' feet, helped the afflicted, and devoted herself to every good work. [11] But refuse to enroll younger widows, for when they are drawn away from Christ by desire, they want to marry [12] and will therefore receive condemnation because they have renounced their original pledge. [13] At the same time, they also learn to be idle, going from house to house; they are not only idle, but are also gossips and busybodies, saying things they shouldn't say. [14] Therefore, I want younger women to marry, have children, manage their households, and give the adversary no opportunity to accuse us. [15] For some have already turned away to follow Satan. [16] If any believing woman has widows in her family, she should help them, and the church should not be burdened, so that it can help those who are genuinely widows.

JAMES 1:27

Pure and undefiled religion before our God and Father is this: to look after orphans and widows in their distress and to keep oneself unstained by the world.

"I WILL NOT LEAVE
YOU AS ORPHANS;
I AM COMING TO YOU."
JOHN 14:18

MAKING ROOM FOR
WIDOWS AND ORPHANS

DATE:

What does Scripture say about making room for widows and orphans?

ISAIAH 1:17

PSALM 68:4–6

JOHN 14:15–18

JAMES 1:27

Why does Scripture urge us to welcome widows and orphans?

How can we make room for both orphans and widows?

Is there a specific person in your life who is an orphan or a widow? Think of that person's name or write it down.

Pray for this person, thanking God that He created every man and woman in His image, giving them worth, value, and dignity. Ask God to help you to show them biblical love and comfort.

MAKING ROOM FOR THE

Stranger

Scripture Reading

———

Leviticus 19:34
Ruth 2:5–12
Matthew 25:35–36
John 4:1–26
Acts 16:6–10

LEVITICUS 19:34

You must regard the foreigner who lives with you as the native-born among you. You are to love him as yourself, for you were foreigners in the land of Egypt; I am Yahweh your God.

RUTH 2:5–12

5 Boaz asked his servant who was in charge of the harvesters, "Whose young woman is this?"

6 The servant answered, "She is the young Moabite woman who returned with Naomi from the land of Moab. 7 She asked, 'Will you let me gather fallen grain among the bundles behind the harvesters?' She came and has remained from early morning until now, except that she rested a little in the shelter."

8 Then Boaz said to Ruth, "Listen, my daughter. Don't go and gather grain in another field, and don't leave this one, but stay here close to my female servants. 9 See which field they are harvesting, and follow them. Haven't I ordered the young men not to touch you? When you are thirsty, go and drink from the jars the young men have filled."

YOU ARE TO LOVE HIM AS YOURSELF, FOR YOU WERE FOREIGNERS IN THE LAND OF EGYPT. LEVITICUS 19:34

[10] She bowed with her face to the ground and said to him, "Why are you so kind to notice me, although I am a foreigner?"

[11] Boaz answered her, "Everything you have done for your mother-in-law since your husband's death has been fully reported to me: how you left your father and mother and the land of your birth, and how you came to a people you didn't previously know. [12] May the LORD reward you for what you have done, and may you receive a full reward from the LORD God of Israel, under whose wings you have come for refuge."

MATTHEW 25:35–36

[35] "For I was hungry
and you gave Me something to eat;
I was thirsty
and you gave Me something to drink;
I was a stranger and you took Me in;
[36] I was naked and you clothed Me;
I was sick and you took care of Me;
I was in prison and you visited Me."

JOHN 4:1–26

JESUS AND THE SAMARITAN WOMAN

[1] When Jesus knew that the Pharisees heard He was making and baptizing more disciples than John [2] (though Jesus Himself was not baptizing, but His disciples were), [3] He left Judea and went again to Galilee. [4] He had to travel through Samaria, [5] so He came to a town of Samaria called Sychar near the property that Jacob had given his son Joseph. [6] Jacob's well was there, and Jesus, worn out from His journey, sat down at the well. It was about six in the evening.

[7] A woman of Samaria came to draw water.

"Give Me a drink," Jesus said to her, [8] for His disciples had gone into town to buy food.

[9] "How is it that You, a Jew, ask for a drink from me, a Samaritan woman?" she asked Him. For Jews do not associate with Samaritans.

[10] Jesus answered, "If you knew the gift of God, and who is saying to you, 'Give Me a drink,' you would ask Him, and He would give you living water."

[11] "Sir," said the woman, "You don't even have a bucket, and the well is deep. So where do You get this 'living water'? [12] You aren't greater than our father Jacob, are You? He gave us the well and drank from it himself, as did his sons and livestock."

[13] Jesus said, "Everyone who drinks from this water will get thirsty again. [14] But whoever drinks from the water that I will give him will never get thirsty again— ever! In fact, the water I will give him will become a well of water springing up within him for eternal life."

[15] "Sir," the woman said to Him, "give me this water so I won't get thirsty and come here to draw water."

[16] "Go call your husband," He told her, "and come back here."

[17] "I don't have a husband," she answered.

"You have correctly said, 'I don't have a husband,'" Jesus said. [18] "For you've had five husbands, and the man you now have is not your husband. What you have said is true."

[19] "Sir," the woman replied, "I see that You are a prophet. [20] Our fathers worshiped on this mountain, yet you Jews say that the place to worship is in Jerusalem."

[21] Jesus told her, "Believe Me, woman, an hour is coming when you will worship the Father neither on this mountain nor in Jerusalem. [22] You Samaritans worship what you do not know. We worship what we do know, because salvation is from the Jews. [23] But an hour is coming, and is now here, when the true worshipers will worship the Father in spirit and truth. Yes, the Father wants such people to worship Him. [24] God is spirit, and those who worship Him must worship in spirit and truth."

[25] The woman said to Him, "I know that Messiah is coming" (who is called Christ). "When He comes, He will explain everything to us."

[26] "I am He," Jesus told her, "the One speaking to you."

ACTS 16:6–10
EVANGELIZATION OF EUROPE

[6] They went through the region of Phrygia and Galatia and were prevented by the Holy Spirit from speaking the message in Asia. [7] When they came to Mysia, they tried to go into Bithynia, but the Spirit of Jesus did not allow them. [8] So, bypassing Mysia, they came down to Troas. [9] During the night a vision appeared to Paul: A Macedonian man was standing and pleading with him, "Cross over to Macedonia and help us!" [10] After he had seen the vision, we immediately made efforts to set out for Macedonia, concluding that God had called us to evangelize them.

MAKING ROOM FOR
THE STRANGER

DATE:

What does Scripture say about making room for strangers?

LEVITICUS 19:34

RUTH 2:5–12

JOHN 4:1–26

ACTS 16:6–10

Why does Scripture urge us to welcome strangers and foreigners?

How can we make room for strangers?

Who is a specific person in your life who is a stranger, refugee, or foreigner? Think of that person's name or write it down.

Pray for this person, thanking God that He created every man and woman in His image, giving them worth, value, and dignity. Ask God to give you a soft heart toward this person and courage to make room for them in your life.

you knit me together

PSALM 139:13

MAKING ROOM FOR

Children

DAY 10

PSALM 139:13–16

13 For it was You who created my inward parts;
You knit me together in my mother's womb.
14 I will praise You
because I have been remarkably and wonderfully made.
Your works are wonderful,
and I know this very well.
15 My bones were not hidden from You
when I was made in secret,
when I was formed in the depths of the earth.
16 Your eyes saw me when I was formless;
all my days were written in Your book and planned
before a single one of them began.

PROVERBS 17:6

Grandchildren are the crown of the elderly,
and the pride of sons is their fathers.

MATTHEW 18:1–6

WHO IS THE GREATEST?

[1] At that time the disciples came to Jesus and said, "Who is greatest in the kingdom of heaven?"

[2] Then He called a child to Him and had him stand among them. [3] "I assure you," He said, "unless you are converted and become like children, you will never enter the kingdom of heaven. [4] Therefore, whoever humbles himself like this child—this one is the greatest in the kingdom of heaven. [5] And whoever welcomes one child like this in My name welcomes Me.

[6] "But whoever causes the downfall of one of these little ones who believe in Me—it would be better for him if a heavy millstone were hung around his neck and he were drowned in the depths of the sea!"

MATTHEW 19:14

Then Jesus said, "Leave the children alone, and don't try to keep them from coming to Me, because the kingdom of heaven is made up of people like this."

MATTHEW 21:14–16

CHILDREN PRAISE JESUS

[14] The blind and the lame came to Him in the temple complex, and He healed them. [15] When the chief priests and the scribes saw the wonders that He did and the children shouting in the temple complex, "Hosanna to the Son of David!" they were indignant [16] and said to Him, "Do You hear what these children are saying?"

"Yes," Jesus told them. "Have you never read:

You have prepared praise
from the mouths of children and nursing infants?"

MARK 10:13–16

BLESSING THE CHILDREN

[13] Some people were bringing little children to Him so He might touch them, but His disciples rebuked them. [14] When Jesus saw it, He was indignant and said to them, "Let the little children come to Me. Don't stop them, for the kingdom of God belongs to such as these. [15] I assure you: Whoever does not welcome the kingdom of God like a little child will never enter it." [16] After taking them in His arms, He laid His hands on them and blessed them.

EPHESIANS 6:1–4

CHILDREN AND PARENTS

[1] Children, obey your parents as you would the Lord, because this is right. [2] Honor your father and mother, which is the first commandment with a promise, [3] so that it may go well with you and that you may have a long life in the land. [4] Fathers, don't stir up anger in your children, but bring them up in the training and instruction of the Lord.

MAKING ROOM FOR **CHILDREN**

DATE:

What does Scripture say about making room for children?

PSALM 139:13–16

MATTHEW 18:1–6

MARK 10:13–16

EPHESIANS 6:1–4

Why does Scripture urge us to welcome children?

How can we make room for children?

Can you think of a specific child or group of children for whom you can make room? Think of their name(s) or write it down.

Pray for this child, thanking God that He created every person in His image, giving them worth, value, and dignity. Ask God to give you a soft heart toward this child and courage to make room for them in your life.

SHOULD I LOVE THIS PERSON?
A FLOWCHART

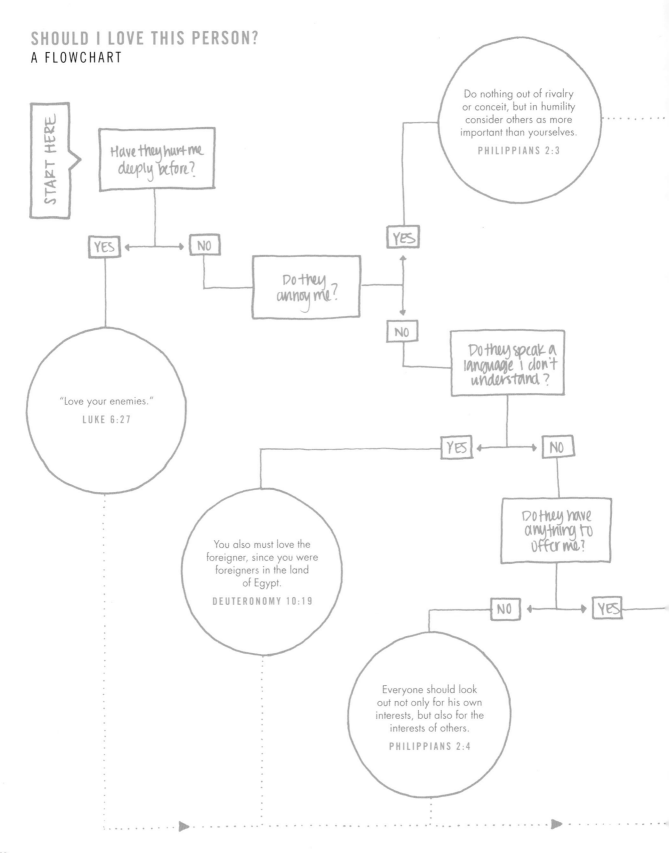

START HERE

Have they hurt me deeply before?

YES — NO

"Love your enemies."
LUKE 6:27

Do they annoy me?

YES

Do nothing out of rivalry or conceit, but in humility consider others as more important than yourselves.
PHILIPPIANS 2:3

NO

Do they speak a language I don't understand?

YES — NO

You also must love the foreigner, since you were foreigners in the land of Egypt.
DEUTERONOMY 10:19

Do they have anything to offer me?

NO — YES

Everyone should look out not only for his own interests, but also for the interests of others.
PHILIPPIANS 2:4

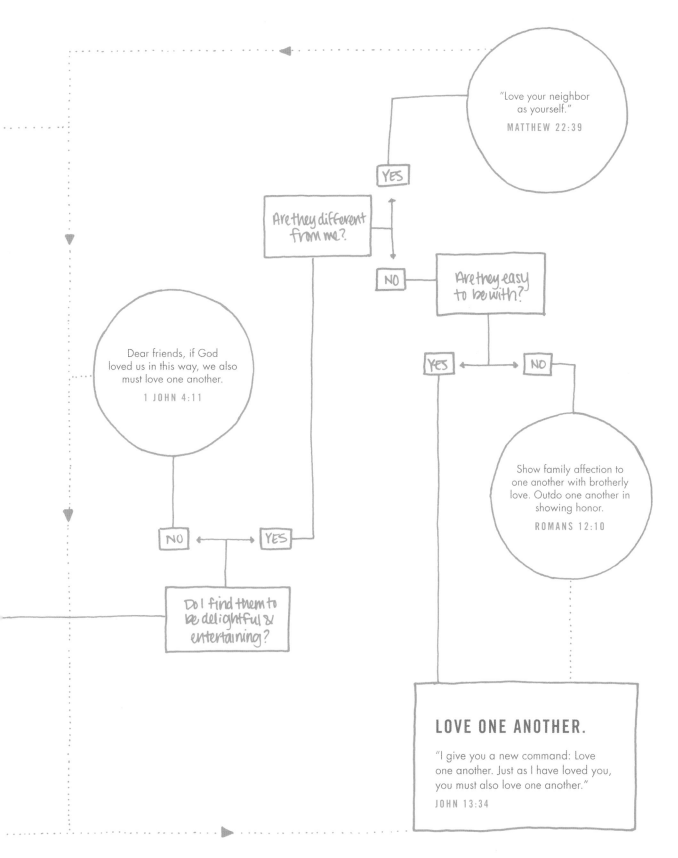

"Love your neighbor as yourself."

MATTHEW 22:39

YES

Are they different from me?

NO

Are they easy to be with?

Dear friends, if God loved us in this way, we also must love one another.

1 JOHN 4:11

YES

NO

Show family affection to one another with brotherly love. Outdo one another in showing honor.

ROMANS 12:10

NO

YES

Do I find them to be delightful & entertaining?

LOVE ONE ANOTHER.

"I give you a new command: Love one another. Just as I have loved you, you must also love one another."

JOHN 13:34

MAKING ROOM FOR THE

Church

PSALM 133:1

How good and pleasant it is
when brothers live together in harmony!

MALACHI 2:10

Don't all of us have one Father? Didn't one God create us? Why then do we act
treacherously against one another, profaning the covenant of our fathers?

JOHN 13:35

"By this all people will know that you are My disciples, if you have love for
one another."

ACTS 4:32

Now the large group of those who believed were of one heart and mind, and no
one said that any of his possessions was his own, but instead they held everything
in common.

ROMANS 8:15–17

[15] For you did not receive a spirit of slavery to fall back into fear, but you received the Spirit of adoption, by whom we cry out, "*Abba*, Father!" [16] The Spirit Himself testifies together with our spirit that we are God's children, [17] and if children, also heirs—heirs of God and coheirs with Christ—seeing that we suffer with Him so that we may also be glorified with Him.

1 CORINTHIANS 12:4–11

[4] Now there are different gifts, but the same Spirit. [5] There are different ministries, but the same Lord. [6] And there are different activities, but the same God activates each gift in each person. [7] A demonstration of the Spirit is given to each person to produce what is beneficial:

[8] to one is given a message of wisdom
through the Spirit,
to another, a message of knowledge
by the same Spirit,
[9] to another, faith by the same Spirit,
to another, gifts of healing by the one Spirit,
[10] to another, the performing of miracles,
to another, prophecy,
to another, distinguishing between spirits,
to another, different kinds of languages,
to another, interpretation of languages.

[11] But one and the same Spirit is active in all these, distributing to each person as He wills.

EPHESIANS 3:8–10

[8] This grace was given to me—the least of all the saints— to proclaim to the Gentiles the incalculable riches of the Messiah, [9] and to shed light for all about the administration of the mystery hidden for ages in God who created all things. [10] This is so God's multi-faceted wisdom may now be made known through the church to the rulers and authorities in the heavens.

COLOSSIANS 3:12–17

THE CHRISTIAN LIFE

[12] Therefore, God's chosen ones, holy and loved, put on heartfelt compassion, kindness, humility, gentleness, and patience, [13] accepting one another and forgiving one another if anyone has a complaint against another. Just as the Lord has forgiven you, so you must also forgive. [14] Above all, put on love—the perfect bond of unity. [15] And let the peace of the Messiah, to which you were also called in one body, control your hearts. Be thankful. [16] Let the message about the Messiah dwell richly among you, teaching and admonishing one another in all wisdom, and singing psalms, hymns, and spiritual songs, with gratitude in your hearts to God. [17] And whatever you do, in word or in deed, do everything in the name of the Lord Jesus, giving thanks to God the Father through Him.

HOW GOOD AND PLEASANT IT IS WHEN BROTHERS LIVE TOGETHER IN HARMONY! PSALM 133:1

MAKING ROOM FOR
THE CHURCH

DATE:

What does Scripture say about making room for the Church?

PSALM 133:1

MALACHI 2:10

ROMANS 8:15–17

COLOSSIANS 3:12–17

Why does Scripture urge us to welcome the Church?

How can we make room for the body of Christ, which is the Church?

Is there a specific person or group of people in the Church whom you struggle to welcome? Think of their name(s), or write it down.

Pray for this person/group, thanking God that He created every man and woman in His image, giving them worth, value, and dignity. Ask God to give you a soft heart toward this person or group, and courage to make room for them in your life.

MAKING ROOM FOR THE

Lost Cause

PSALM 25:3

No one who waits for You
will be disgraced;
those who act treacherously without cause
will be disgraced.

PSALM 28:6–9

6 May the LORD be praised,
for He has heard the sound of my pleading.
7 The LORD is my strength and my shield;
my heart trusts in Him, and I am helped.
Therefore my heart rejoices,
and I praise Him with my song.

8 The LORD is the strength of His people;
He is a stronghold of salvation for His anointed.
9 Save Your people, bless Your possession,
shepherd them, and carry them forever.

"TODAY SALVATION HAS COME TO THIS HOUSE," JESUS TOLD HIM, "BECAUSE HE TOO IS A SON OF ABRAHAM. FOR THE SON OF MAN HAS COME TO SEEK AND TO SAVE THE LOST." LUKE 19:9–10

JONAH 3

JONAH'S PREACHING

[1] Then the word of the Lᴏʀᴅ came to Jonah a second time: [2] "Get up! Go to the great city of Nineveh and preach the message that I tell you." [3] So Jonah got up and went to Nineveh according to the Lᴏʀᴅ's command.

Now Nineveh was an extremely large city, a three-day walk. [4] Jonah set out on the first day of his walk in the city and proclaimed, "In 40 days Nineveh will be demolished!" [5] The men of Nineveh believed in God. They proclaimed a fast and dressed in sackcloth—from the greatest of them to the least.

[6] When word reached the king of Nineveh, he got up from his throne, took off his royal robe, put on sackcloth, and sat in ashes. [7] Then he issued a decree in Nineveh:

By order of the king and his nobles: No man or beast, herd or flock, is to taste anything at all. They must not eat or drink water. [8] Furthermore, both man and beast must be covered with sackcloth, and everyone must call out earnestly to God. Each must turn from his evil ways and from the violence he is doing. [9] Who knows? God may turn and relent; He may turn from His burning anger so that we will not perish.

[10] Then God saw their actions—that they had turned from their evil ways—so God relented from the disaster He had threatened to do to them. And He did not do it.

LUKE 19:1-10

JESUS VISITS ZACCHAEUS

¹ He entered Jericho and was passing through. ² There was a man named Zacchaeus who was a chief tax collector, and he was rich. ³ He was trying to see who Jesus was, but he was not able because of the crowd, since he was a short man. ⁴ So running ahead, he climbed up a sycamore tree to see Jesus, since He was about to pass that way. ⁵ When Jesus came to the place, He looked up and said to him, "Zacchaeus, hurry and come down because today I must stay at your house."

⁶ So he quickly came down and welcomed Him joyfully. ⁷ All who saw it began to complain, "He's gone to lodge with a sinful man!"

⁸ But Zacchaeus stood there and said to the Lord, "Look, I'll give half of my possessions to the poor, Lord! And if I have extorted anything from anyone, I'll pay back four times as much!"

⁹ "Today salvation has come to this house," Jesus told him, "because he too is a son of Abraham. ¹⁰ For the Son of Man has come to seek and to save the lost."

ACTS 9:17-31

¹⁷ So Ananias left and entered the house. Then he placed his hands on him and said, "Brother Saul, the Lord Jesus, who appeared to you on the road you were traveling, has sent me so that you can regain your sight and be filled with the Holy Spirit."

¹⁸ At once something like scales fell from his eyes, and he regained his sight. Then he got up and was baptized. ¹⁹ And after taking some food, he regained his strength.

SAUL PROCLAIMING THE MESSIAH

Saul was with the disciples in Damascus for some days. ²⁰ Immediately he began proclaiming Jesus in the synagogues: "He is the Son of God."

²¹ But all who heard him were astounded and said, "Isn't this the man who, in Jerusalem, was destroying those who called on this name and then came here for the purpose of taking them as prisoners to the chief priests?"

²² But Saul grew more capable and kept confounding the Jews who lived in Damascus by proving that this One is the Messiah.

²³ After many days had passed, the Jews conspired to kill him, ²⁴ but their plot became known to Saul. So they were watching the gates day and night intending to kill him, ²⁵ but his disciples took him by night and lowered him in a large basket through an opening in the wall.

SAUL IN JERUSALEM

²⁶ When he arrived in Jerusalem, he tried to associate with the disciples, but they were all afraid of him, since they did not believe he was a disciple. ²⁷ Barnabas, however, took him and brought him to the apostles and explained to them how Saul had seen the Lord on the road and that He had talked to him, and how in Damascus he had spoken boldly in the name of Jesus. ²⁸ Saul was coming and going with them in Jerusalem, speaking boldly in the name of the Lord. ²⁹ He conversed and debated with the Hellenistic Jews, but they attempted to kill him. ³⁰ When the brothers found out, they took him down to Caesarea and sent him off to Tarsus.

³¹ So the church throughout all Judea, Galilee, and Samaria had peace, being built up and walking in the fear of the Lord and in the encouragement of the Holy Spirit, and it increased in numbers.

1 PETER 2:9

But you are a chosen race, a royal priesthood,
a holy nation, a people for His possession,
so that you may proclaim the praises of the
One who called you out of darkness into
His marvelous light.

MAKING ROOM FOR
THE LOST CAUSE

DATE:

What does Scripture say about making
room for the lost cause?

PSALM 25:3

JONAH 3

ACTS 9:17–31

1 PETER 2:9

Why does Scripture urge us to welcome
those who seem beyond reach of
the gospel?

How can we make room for those who
seem to be lost causes?

Who is a specific person in your life you
have written off as a lost cause? Think of
that person's name or write it down.

Pray for this person, thanking God that He created every man
and woman in His image, giving them worth, value, and dignity.
Ask God to give you a soft heart toward this person, and pray
for mutual humility, restoration, and repentance.

DAY 13
GRACE DAY

DATE:

Take this day as an opportunity to catch up on your reading,
pray, and rest in the presence of the Lord.

For I was hungry AND you gave me food, I was thirsty AND you gave me drink, I was a stranger AND you welcomed me.

Matthew 25:35 ESV

DAY 14
WEEKLY TRUTH

DATE:

Memorizing Scripture is one of the best ways to carry God-breathed truth, instruction, and reproof wherever we go.

In this study of hospitality we are memorizing Romans 15:5–7, a passage that focuses on glorifying God and living in harmony with one another. This week we will memorize verse 7.

THEREFORE WELCOME ONE ANOTHER AS CHRIST HAS WELCOMED YOU, FOR THE GLORY OF GOD.

ROMANS 15:7 ESV

Punch out the memory card for this passage in the back of your book and place it somewhere you'll see it often. As you memorize this verse, give thanks to God for the gift of His Word.

Where did I study?

- ○ HOME
- ○ CHURCH
- ○ A FRIEND'S HOUSE
- ○ SCHOOL
- ○ COFFEE SHOP
- ○ OTHER

DID I LISTEN TO MUSIC?

ARTIST:

SONG:

SCRIPTURE I WILL
SHARE WITH A FRIEND:

WHEN DID I HAVE MY BEST STUDYING SUCCESS?

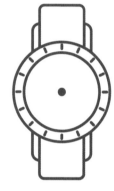

WHAT WAS HAPPENING IN THE WORLD?

What was my best takeaway?

WHAT WAS MY BIGGEST FEAR?   ▷   What was my greatest comfort?

I LEARNED THESE UNEXPECTED NEW THINGS:

1

2

3

END DATE

| MONTH | DAY | YEAR |

BIBLIOGRAPHY

Homan, Daniel, and Lonni Collins Pratt. *Radical Hospitality: Benedict's Way of Love.* Brewster, MA: Paraclete Press, 2002.
Nouwen, Henri J. M. *Reaching Out: The Three Movements of the Spiritual Life.* Garden City, NY: Doubleday, 1975.

COLOPHON

This book was printed offset in Nashville, Tennessee, on 70# Lynx Opaque. Typefaces used include Trade Gothic, Garamond, and Euclid. Cover is printed offset on Tango 12pt C1S with a soft-touch matte laminate. Finished size is 8"x10".

EDITORS-IN-CHIEF: Raechel Myers and Amanda Bible Williams

MANAGING EDITOR: Rebecca Faires

EDITOR: Russ Ramsey

CREATIVE DIRECTOR: Ryan Myers

ART DIRECTOR: Amanda Barnhart

LETTERING: Cymone Wilder

ILLUSTRATION & PRODUCTION DESIGN: Kelsea Allen

THEOLOGICAL OVERSIGHT:
Russ Ramsey, MDiv., ThM.
and Nate Shurden, MDiv.

COMMUNITY CORRESPONDENT: Kaitlin Wernet

COVER PHOTOGRAPHER: Cymone Wilder

PHOTOGRAPHY: Ashley Glass, Kellie Beth Scott, Alyssa Valletta

EDITORIAL INTERN: Savannah Summers

SUBSCRIPTION INQUIRIES:
orders@shereadstruth.com

She Reads Truth is a worldwide community of women who
read God's Word together every day.

Founded in 2012, She Reads Truth invites women of all ages
to engage with Scripture through daily reading plans, online
conversation led by a vibrant community of contributors,
and offline resources created at the intersection of beauty,
goodness, and Truth.

STOP BY

shereadstruth.com

SHOP

shopshereadstruth.com

KEEP IN TOUCH

@shereadstruth

📷 🐦 f

DOWNLOAD THE APP

SEND A NOTE

hello@shereadstruth.com

SHARE

#SheReadsTruth